ORESTES
Voltaire
Translation by William F. Fleming

Start Publishing PD LLC
Copyright © 2024 by Start Publishing PD LLC

All rights reserved, including the right to reproduce this book or portions thereof in any form whatsoever.

Start Publishing PD is a registered trademark of Start Publishing PD LLC
Manufactured in the United States of America

Cover art: Shutterstock/Taisiya Kozorez

Cover design: Jennifer Do

10 9 8 7 6 5 4 3 2 1

ISBN 979-8-8809-0934-6

Contents

Dramatis Personæ. 4
Act I. 7
Act II. 16
Act III. 25
Act IV. 36
Act V. 44

DRAMATIS PERSONÆ.

Ægisthus.
Orestes, Son of Agamemnon and Clytemnæstra.
Electra, Sisters of Orestes.
IPHISA, Sisters of Orestes.
ClytemnÆstra, Wife of Ægisthus.
Pylades, Friend of Orestes.
Pammenes, an old Man, attached to the Family of Agamemnon.
Dimas, an Officer of the Guards.
Attendants.

Orestes was produced in 1750, an experiment which intensely interested the literary world and the public. In his Dedicatory Letters to the Duchess of Maine, Voltaire has the following passage on the Greek drama:

"We should not, I acknowledge, endeavor to imitate what is weak and defective in the ancients: it is most probable that their faults were well known to their contemporaries. I am satisfied, Madam, that the wits of Athens condemned, as well as you, some of those repetitions, and some declamations with which Sophocles has loaded his *Electra*: they must have observed that he had not dived deep enough into the human heart. I will moreover fairly confess, that there are beauties peculiar not only to the Greek language, but to the climate, to manners and times, which it would be ridiculous to transplant hither. Therefore I have not copied exactly the *Electra* of Sophocles—much more I knew would be necessary; but I have taken, as well as I could, all the spirit and substance of it. The feast celebrated by Ægisthus and Clytemnæstra, which they called the feast of Agamemnon; the arrival of Orestes and Pylades; the urn which was supposed to contain the ashes of Orestes; the ring of Agamemnon; the character of Electra, and that of Iphisa, which is exactly the Chrysothemis of Sophocles; and above all, the remorse of Clytemnæstra; these I have copied from the Greek tragedy. When the messenger, who relates the fictitious story of the death of Orestes, says to Clytemnæstra: 'I see, Madam, you are deeply affected by his death;' she replies, 'I am a mother, and must therefore be unhappy; a mother, though injured, cannot hate her own offspring:' she even endeavors to justify herself to Electra, with regard to the murder of Agamemnon, and laments her daughter. Euripides has carried Clytemnæstra's repentance still further. This, Madam, was what gained the applause of the most judicious and sensible people upon earth, and was approved by all good judges in our own nation. No character, in reality, can be more natural than that of a woman, criminal with regard to her husband, yet softened by her children; a woman, whose proud and fiery disposition is still open to pity and compassion, who resumes the fierceness of her character on receiving too severe reproaches, and at last sinks into submission and tears. The seeds of this character were in Sophocles and Euripides, and I have only unfolded them. Nothing but ignorance, and its natural attendant, presumption, can assert that the ancients have nothing worthy of our imitation: there is scarcely one real and essential beauty and perfection, for the foundation of which, at least, we are not indebted to them.

"I have taken particular care not to depart from that simplicity so strongly recommended by the Greeks, and so difficult to attain; the true mark of genius and invention, and the very essence of all theatrical merit. A foreign character, brought into *Œdipus* or *Electra*, who should play a principal part and draw aside the attention of the audience, would be a monster in the eyes of all those who have any knowledge of the ancients, or of that nature which they have so finely painted. Art and genius consist in finding everything within the subject, and never going out of it in search of additional ornaments: but how are we to imitate that truly tragic pomp and magnificence which we find in the verses of Sophocles, that natural elegance and purity of diction, without which the piece, howsoever well conducted in other respects, must after all be but a poor performance!

"I have at least given my countrymen some idea of a tragedy without love, without confidants, and without episodes: the few partisans of good taste acknowledge themselves obliged to me for it, though the rest of the world withhold their approbation for a time, but will come in at last, when the rage of party is over, the injustice of persecution at an end, and the clouds of ignorance dissipated. You, Madam, must preserve among us those glittering sparks of light which the ancients have transmitted to us; we owe everything to them: not an art was born among us: everything was transplanted: but the earth that bears these foreign fruits is worn out, and our ancient barbarism, by the help of false taste, would break out again in spite of all our culture and improvement: and the disciples of Athens and Rome become Goths and Vandals, corrupted with the manners of the Sybarites, without the kind favor and protection of persons of your rank. When nature has given them either genius, or the love of genius, they encourage this nation, which is better able to imitate than to invent; and which always looks up towards the great for those instructions and examples which it perpetually stands in need of. All that I wish for, Madam, is, that some genius may be found to finish what I have but just sketched out; to free the stage from that effeminacy and affectation which it is now sunk into; to render it respectable to the gravest characters; worthy of the few great masterpieces which we already have among us; worthy, in short, the approbation of a mind like yours, and all those who may hereafter endeavor to resemble you."

ACT I.

SCENE I.

Scene, the seashore, a wood, a temple, a palace and a tomb, on one side: on the other, Argos at a distance.

Iphisa, Pammenes.

Iphisa: Sayest thou, Pammenes? shall these hated walls, Where I so long have dragged a life of woe, Afford at least the melancholy comfort Of mingling sorrow with my dear Electra? And will Ægisthus bring her to the tomb Of Agamemnon, bring his daughter here, To be a witness of the horrid pomp, The sad solemnity, which on this day Annual returns, to celebrate their crimes, And make their guilt immortal?

Pammenes: O Iphisa, Thou honored daughter of my royal master, Like thee, confined within these lonely walls, The secrets of a vile abandoned court Do seldom reach Pammenes; but, 'tis rumored, The jealous tyrant brings Electra here, Fearful lest Argos, by her cries alarmed, Should rise to vengeance; every heart, he knows, Feels for the injured princess, therefore much He dreads her clamors; with a watchful eye Observes her conduct, treats her as a slave, And leads the captive to adorn his triumph.

Iphisa: Good heaven! and must Electra be a slave! Shall Agamemnon's blood be thus disgraced By a barbarian? Will her cruel mother, Will Clytemnæstra bear the vile reproach That on herself recoils, and all her race? Perhaps my sister is too fierce of soul, She mingles too much pride and bitterness Of keen resentment with her griefs; alas! Weak are her arms against a tyrant's power: What will her anger, what her pride avail her? They only irritate a haughty foe, And cannot serve our cause: my fate at least Is milder, and this solitary state Shields me from wrongs which must oppress Electra. Far from my father's foes, these pious hands Can pay due offerings to his honored shade: Far from his murderer, in this sad retreat Freely I weep in peace, and curse Ægisthus: I'm not condemned to see the tyrant here, Save when the Sun unwillingly brings round The fatal day that knit the dreadful tie, When that inhuman monster shed the blood Of Agamemnon, when base Clytemnæstra—

SCENE II.

Electra, Iphisa, Pammenes.

Iphisa: O my Electra! art thou here? my sister—

Electra: The day of horror is returned, Iphisa: The dreadful rites, the guilty feast prepared, Have brought me hither; thy Electra comes, Thy captive sister, comes a wretched slave, To bear the tidings of their guilty joy.

Iphisa: To see Electra is a blessing still, It pours some joy into the bitter cup Of sorrow, thus to mix my tears with thine.

Electra: Tears, my Iphisa! I have shed enough Of them already: O thou bleeding ghost Of my dead father, ever-honored shade, Is that the tribute which I owe to thee? I owe thee blood, and blood thou hast required; Amidst the pomp of this dire festival, Dragged by Ægisthus here, I will collect My scattered spirits, shake off these vile chains, And be my own avenger: yes, Iphisa, This feeble arm shall reach the tyrant's heart: Did not the cruel Clytemnæstra shed A husband's blood? did I not see her lift Her barbarous hand against him, and shall we Suspend the blow, and let a murderer live? O vengeance, and thou, animating virtue, That dost inspire me, art thou not as bold As daring guilt? we must revenge ourselves, We must, Iphisa: fearest thou then to strike, Fearest thou to die? shall Clytemnæstra's daughter, The blood of Atreus fear? O rather lend Thy aid, and join the desperate Electra!

Iphisa: My dearest sister, moderate thy rage, And calm thy troubled mind: against our foes What can we bring but unavailing tears? Who will assist us? who will lend us arms? Or how shall we surprise a watchful king, For guilt is ever fearful, by his guards Surrounded? why, Electra, wilt thou court Perpetual danger? should the tyrant hear Thy loud complaints, I tremble for thy life.

Electra: Why let him hear them? I would have my grief Sink to his heart, and poison all his joys: Yes; I would have my cries ascend to heaven, And bring the thunder down; would have them raise A hundred kings, who never yet have dared, Unworthy cowards as they are, to avenge Great Agamemnon. but I pardon thee, And the vain terrors of thy fearful soul, That shrinks at danger; for he favors you, I know he does, and only crushes me Beneath his iron yoke: thou hast not been, Like me, a wretched persecuted slave; Thou didst not see the impious parricide, The horrid[1] feast, the dire solemnity, When Clytemnæstra—O the dreadful image Is still before me, in this place, Iphisa, Where now thou tremblest to declare thy wrongs, There did these eyes behold our hapless father Caught in the deadly snare: Pammenes heard His dying groans, and ran with me to save him: But when I came, what did I see! my mother Plunging her ruthless dagger in his breast, To rob him of the poor remains of life. [Turning to Pammenes.] Thou sawest me take Orestes in my arms, My dear Orestes; little knew he then Of danger, but as near his murdered father He stood, called out for aid to Clytemnæstra: She, midst the horrors of the guilty scene, Stopped for a moment short, and gave us time Safe to convey the victim from Ægisthus. Whether the tyrant has completed yet The imperfect vengeance in Orestes' blood, I know not: O my brother, dost thou live, Or hast thou followed thy unhappy father? Alas! I weep for him, and fear for thee. These hands are loaded with inglorious chains, And these sad eyes, forever bathed in tears, See naught but guilt, oppression, and despair.

Pammenes: Ye dear remains of Atreus' honored race, Whose splendor I have seen, whose woes I feel, Permit a friend to fill your weeping souls With cheerful hope, that ever waits propitious To soothe affliction: call to mind what heaven Long since hath promised, that its vengeful hand Should one day lead Orestes to the place Where we preserved him; that Ægisthus there, Even at yon tomb, and on the fatal day Marked for his impious triumph o'er the dead, Should pay the forfeit of his crime: the Gods Can ne'er deceive; in darkness still they veil Their secret purpose from the eyes of men, And punishment with slow but certain steps, Still follows guilt.

Iphisa: But wherefore stays so long Their tardy vengeance? I have languished here In grief and anguish many a tedious hour; Electra, still more wretched, is in chains: Meantime the proud oppressor lives in peace, And glories in his crimes.

Electra: Thou seest, Pammenes, Ægisthus still renews his cruel triumph, And celebrates the fatal nuptials; still A wretched exile lives my dear Orestes, Forgetful of his father, and Electra.

Pammenes: But mark the course of time: he touches now The age when manly strength, with courage joined, May aid your purpose; hope for his return, And trust in heaven.

Electra: We will: thou son of wisdom, Thou good old man, O thou hast darted forth A ray of hope on my despairing soul! If with unpitying eye the gods beheld Our miseries here, and proud oppression, still Unpunished, trampled on the tender feet Of innocence, what hand would crown their altars With incense and oblation! but kind heaven Will give Orestes to a sister's arms, And blast the tyrant: hear my voice, Orestes, O hear thy country's, hear the cries of blood, That call thee forth; come from thy dreary caves, And pathless deserts, where misfortune long Hath tried thy courage; leave thy savage prey, And all the roaming monsters of the forest, To chase the beasts of Argos, to destroy The tyrants of the earth, the murderers Of kings; O haste, and let me guide thy hand Even to the traitor's breast.

Iphisa: No more: repress Thy griefs, Electra; see, thy mother comes.

Electra: And have I yet a mother?

SCENE III.

Clytemnæstra, Electra, Iphisa.

Clytemnæstra: Hence, and leave me; You may retire, Pammenes; stay, my daughters.

Iphisa: Alas! that sacred name dispels my fears.

Electra: And doubles mine.

Clytemnæstra: Touching your fate, my children, I came to lay a mother's heart before you. Barren, thank heaven, hath been my second bed, Nor brought a race of jealous foes to sow Division here. Alas! my little race Is almost run; the secret grief that long Hath preyed on my sad heart will finish soon A life of woe: spite of Ægisthus, still I love my children; spite of all his rage, Electra, thou who in thy infant years So oft hast given me comfort, when the loss Of Iphigenia, and her cruel father Oppressed my soul; though now thy pride disdains me,

And braves my power, thou art my daughter still; Unworthy as thou art, there's still a place In Clytemnæstra's heart for her Electra.

Electra: For me! O heaven, and am I yet beloved; And dost thou feel for thy unhappy daughter? O, if thou dost, behold her chains, behold Yon tomb—

Clytemnæstra: Unkind Electra, thus to wake The sad remembrance! thou hast plunged a dagger Into thy mother's breast; but I deserve it.

Electra: Thou hast disarmed Electra, nature pleads A mother's cause; I own myself to blame For all the bitterness of sorrow poured In dreadful execrations on thy head. By thee delivered to the tyrant's power, I would have torn thee from him; I lament, But cannot hate thee. O, if gracious heaven Hath touched thy soul with wholesome penitence, Obey its sacred will, and hear the voice Of conscience, that commands thee to unloose The horrid ties that bind thee to a wretch Despised and hated; follow the great God Who leads thy footsteps to the paths of virtue; Call back your son, let him return to fill The throne of his great ancestors, to scourge A tyrant, to avenge his murdered father, His sisters, and his mother: haste and send For my Orestes.

Clytemnæstra: Talk no more of that, Electra, nor speak thus of my Ægisthus: I grieve to see thee in these shameful bonds; But know, a sovereign cannot tamely brook Repeated insults, or embrace a foe: You had provoked him to, be cruel; I, Who am but his first subject, oft have tried To soothe his anger, but in vain: my words, Instead of healing, but inflamed the wound: Electra is indebted to herself For all her deep-felt injuries; henceforth bend To thy condition; let thy sister teach thee That we must yield submissive to our fate, If e'er we hope to change it. I could wish To end my days in peace amongst my children; But if thy rapid and imprudent zeal Should bring Orestes here before the time, His life might answer for it, and thy own, If the king see him: though I pity thee, Electra, yet I owe a husband more Than a lost son, whom I have cause to fear.

Electra: O heaven, that monster! he thy husband, he! And is it thus thou pitiest me? alas, What will this poor, this light remorse avail thee, This fleeting sorrow? was thy tenderness But for a moment, dost thou threaten me, [To Iphisa.] Is this, Iphisa, this a mother's love? [To Clytemnæstra.] It seems thou threatenest my Orestes too; Thou hast no cause to fear, nor I to hope For him:

alas! perhaps he is no more; Perhaps Ægisthus, the detested tyrant, He whom but now thou didst not blush to call Thy husband, hath in secret ta'en his life.

Iphisa: Believe me, Madam, when I call the gods To witness, poor Electra and myself Are strangers to the fate of dear Orestes; Have pity then on your afflicted daughter, Pity your helpless son and spare Electra: She has been wronged; her tears and her reproaches Suit well her fate, and ought to be forgiven.

Electra: I must not hope it, must not even complain; And if Orestes lives but in my thoughts 'Tis deemed a crime. I know Ægisthus well, Know his fierce nature; if he fears my brother, He'll soon destroy him.

Clytemnæstra: Know, thy brother lives; If he's in danger, 'tis from thy imprudence; Therefore be humble, moderate thy transports, Respect thy mother: thinkest thou I come here, Elate with joy, to lead the splendid triumph? O no, to me it is a day of sorrow; Thou weepest in chains, and I upon a throne. I know the cruel vows thy hatred made Against me: O, Electra! cease thy prayers, The gods have heard thee but too well already: Retire, and leave me.

SCENE IV. **Clytemnæstra**: [Alone.] How it shocks my soul To see my children! O the guilty bed! My fatal marriage, and long prosperous crimes, Adultery and murder, horrid bonds! How ye torment me now! my little dream Of happiness is o'er, and conscience darts Its sudden rays on my affrighted soul. How can Ægisthus live so long in peace! Fearless he leads me on to share with him These cruel triumphs; but my spirits fail, My strength forsakes me, and I tremble now At every omen; fear my subjects, fear All Argos, Greece, Electra, and Orestes. How dreadful 'tis to hate the blood that flowed Congenial with our own, to dread the names Which mortals hold so sacred and so dear! But injured nature, banished from my heart, Indignant frowns, and to avenge herself Now bids me tremble at the name of son.

SCENE V.

Ægisthus, Clytemnæstra.

Clytemnæstra: Cruel Ægisthus, wherefore wouldst thou lead me To this sad place, the seat of death and horror?

Ægisthus: Is then the solemn pomp, the feast of joy, The sweet remembrance of our prosperous days, Grown hateful to thee? is our marriage day A day of horror?

Clytemnæstra: No: but here, Ægisthus, There may be danger: my unhappy children Have filled this heart with anguish: poor Iphisa Weeps her hard lot; Electra is in chains; This fatal place reminds me of the blood We shed, reminds me of my dear Orestes, Of Agamemnon.

Ægisthus: Let Iphisa weep, And proud Electra rave; I bore too long Her bitter taunts, 'tis fit her haughtiness Should now be humbled; I'll not suffer her To stir up foul rebellion in my kingdom, To tell the factions that Orestes comes, And call down vengeance on me; every hour That hated name is echoed in my ear, I must not bear it.

Clytemnæstra: Ha! what name was that? Orestes! O, I shudder at the thought Of his approach: an oracle long since Declared, that here, even at the fatal tomb Whither thou leadest, his parricidal hand Should one day rise vindictive, and destroy us. Why therefore wouldst thou tempt the gods, why thus Expose a life so dear to Clytemnæstra?

Ægisthus: Be not alarmed; Orestes ne'er shall hurt thee: His be the danger; for I have sent forth Some friends in search of him, and soon I hope Shall see him in the toils; a wretched exile From clime to clime he roams, and now it seems In Epidaurus' gloomy forest hides His ignominious head; but there perhaps We have more friends than Clytemnæstra thinks of; The king may serve us.

Clytemnæstra: But, my son—

Ægisthus: I know He's fierce, implacable, revengeful; stung By his misfortunes, all the blood of Atreus Boils in his breast, and animates his rage.

Clytemnæstra: Alas! my lord, his rage is but too just.

Ægisthus: Be it our business then to make it vain; Thou knowest I've sent my Plisthenes in secret To Epidaurus.

Clytemnæstra: But for what?

Ægisthus: To fix My throne in safety, and remove thy fears: Yes, Plisthenes, my son, by thee adopted Heir to my kingdom, knows too well how much His interest must depend on the event E'er to neglect his charge: he is thy son, Think of no other: had Electra's heart Submissive yielded to another's counsels, She had been happy in my Plisthenes: But she shall feel the power which she contemns, She and her haughty brother, her Orestes, He may be found perhaps.—You seem disturbed.

Clytemnæstra: Alas! Ægisthus, must we sacrifice More victims? must I purchase length of days With added guilt? Thou knowest whose blood we shed— And must my son too perish, must I pay So dear a price for life?

Ægisthus: Remember—

Clytemnæstra: No: First let me ask the sacred oracle—

Ægisthus: What canst thou hope from gods or oracles, Were they consulted on the blissful day That gave Ægisthus to his Clytemnæstra?

Clytemnæstra: Thou hast recalled a time when heaven, I fear, Was much offended: love defies the gods, But fear adores them; guilt weighs down my soul, Do not oppress my feeble spirits; time, That changes all, hath altered this proud heart; The hand of heaven is on me, and subdues The haughty rage that once inspired my breast; Not that my tender friendship for Ægisthus Can e'er decay, our interests are the same; But to behold my daughter made a slave, To think on my poor lost abandoned son, To think that now, even now, perhaps he dies By vile assassins, or, if living, lives My foe, and hates the guilty Clytemnæstra, Is it not dreadful? pity me, Ægisthus, I am a mother still.

Ægisthus: Thou art my wife; Thou art my queen; resume thy wonted courage, And be thyself again; indulge no more This foolish fondness for ungrateful children, Who merit not thy love; consult alone Ægisthus' safety, and thy own repose.

Clytemnæstra: Repose! the guilty mind can ne'er enjoy it.

ACT II.

SCENE I.

Orestes, Pylades.

Orestes: Whither, my Pylades, hath cruel fate Conducted us? alas! Orestes lives But to increase the sorrows of his friend: Our arms, our treasures, and our soldiers lost In the rude storm; here on this desert coast, No succor near, deserted and forlorn We wander on, and naught but hope remains. Where are we?

Pylades: That I know not; but since fate Hath led us hither, let us not despair; It is enough for me, Orestes lives: Be confident; the barbarous Ægisthus In vain pursued thy life, which heaven preserved In Epidaurus, when thy arm subdued The gallant Plisthenes: let naught alarm Or terrify thy soul, but boldly urge Thy way, protected by that guardian God Who watches o'er the just, the great avenger, Who hath already to thy valor given The son, and promised that ere long the father Shall follow him.

Orestes: Alas, my friend, that God In anger now withdraws his powerful aid, And frowns upon us, as thy cruel fate Too plainly shows; a terrible example! But say, within the rock didst thou conceal The urn, which to Mycenæ, horrid seat Of murder, by the gods command, we bear; That urn which holds the ashes of my foe, Of Plisthenes; with that we must deceive The tyrant.

Pylades: I have done it.

Orestes: Gracious heaven! When shall we reap the fruits of our obedience? When will the wished-for day of vengeance come? Shall I again behold my native soil, The dear, the dreadful place where first I saw The light of day? Where, shall I find my sister, The pride, the glory, of admiring Greece; That generous maid, whom all unite to praise, But none will dare to succor? She preserved My life; and, worthy of her noble father, Hath never bent beneath the oppressive hand Of power, but braved the fury of the storm. How many kings, how many heroes, fought For Menelaus! Agamemnon dies, And Greece forgets him, whilst his hapless son, Deserted, wanders o'er a faithless world, To seek some blest asylum for repose. Alas, without thy friendship I had been The most distressed, most abject of mankind: But heaven, in pity to my woes, hath sent My Pylades; it would not let me perish, But gave me to subdue my hated foe, And half avenge my father: say, my friend, What path will lead us to the tyrant's court?

Pylades: Behold that palace, and the towering height Of yon proud temple, the dark grove overgrown With cypress, and the tomb, rich images Of mournful splendor all: and see! this way Advancing, comes a venerable sage, Of mildest aspect, and whose years, no doubt, Have long experience of calamity; His soul will melt at thy disastrous fate.

Orestes: Is every mortal born to suffer? hark! He groans, my Pylades.

SCENE II.

Orestes, Pylades, Pammenes.

Pylades: Whoe'er thou art, Stop, and inform us: we are strangers here. Two poor unhappy friends, long time the sport Of winds and waves, now on this unknown shore Cast helpless, canst thou tell us if this place Will be or fatal to us, or propitious?

Pammenes: I am a simple, plain old man, and here Worship the gods, adore their justice, live In humble fear of them, and exercise The sacred rights of hospitality; Ye both are welcome to my little cottage, There to despise with me the pride of kings, Their pomp and riches; come, my friends, for such I ever hold the wretched.

Orestes: Generous stranger, May gracious heaven inspire us with the means To recompense thy goodness! but inform us What place is this; who is your king?

Pammenes: Ægisthus: I am his subject.

Orestes: Terrors, crimes, and vengeance! O heaven, Ægisthus!

Pylades: Soft: do not betray us; Be careful.

Orestes: Gods, Ægisthus! he who murdered—

Pammenes: The same.

Orestes: And Clytemnæstra, lives she still After that fatal blow.

Pammenes: She reigns with him; The rest is known too well.

Orestes: That tomb before us, And yonder palace—

Pammenes: Is inhabited Now by Ægisthus; built, I well remember, By worthier hands, and for a better use. The tomb thou seest, forgive me if I weep At the remembrance, is the tomb of him I loved, my lord, my king—of Agamemnon.

Orestes: O 'tis too much! I sink beneath it.

Pylades: Hide Thy tears, my friend. [To Orestes, who turns away from him.]

Pammenes: You seem much moved, and fain Would stop the tide of grief: O give it way, Indulge thy sorrows, and lament the son Of gods, the noble conqueror of Troy; Whilst they insult his sacred memory here, Strangers shall weep the fate of Agamemnon.

Orestes: A stranger as I am, I cannot look With cold indifference on the noble race Of Atreus, 'tis a Grecian's duty ever To weep the fate of heroes, and I ought— But doth Electra live in Argos still?

Pammenes: She doth, she's here.

Orestes: I run, I fly to meet her.

Pylades: Ha! whither wouldst thou go! What! brave the gods Hazard thy precious life! forbear, my lord. [To Pammenes.] O, sir, conduct us to the neighboring temple, There will we lay our gifts before the altar In humble duty, and adore that God Who ruled the waves, and saved us from destruction.

Orestes: Wilt thou conduct us to the sacred tomb Where lie the ashes of a murdered hero? There must I offer to his honored shade A secret sacrifice.

Pammenes: O heavenly justice, Thou sacrifice to him! amidst his foes! O noble youth! my master had a son, Who, in Electra's arms—but I forbear, Ægisthus comes: away; I'll follow you.

Orestes: Ægisthus! ha!

Pylades: We must avoid his presence.

SCENE III.

Ægisthus, Clytemnæstra, Pammenes.

Ægisthus: [To Pammenes] Who are those strangers? one of them methought Seemed, by his stately port and fair demeanor, Of noble birth, a gloom of melancholy Hangs on his brow: he struck me as he passed: Is he our subject? knowest thou whence he came?

Pammenes: I only know they are unfortunate; Driven by the tempest on those rocks, they came For shelter here; as strangers I relieved them; It was my duty: if they tell me truth, Greece is their country.

Ægisthus: Thou shalt answer for them On peril of thy life.

Clytemnæstra: Alas! my lord, Can these poor objects raise suspicion?

Ægisthus: Yes: The people murmur; everything alarms me.

Clytemnæstra: Such for these fifteen years hath been our fate, To fear, and to be feared; the bitter poison To all my happiness.

Ægisthus: Away, Pammenes; Let me know who and whence they are; why thus They come so near the palace; from what port Their vessel sailed, and wherefore on the seas Where I command: away, and bring me word.

SCENE IV.

Ægisthus, Clytemnæstra.

Ægisthus: Well, madam, to remove thy idle fears, The interpreters of heaven it seems at length Have been consulted; but in vain: their silence Doubles thy grief, and heightens thy despair; For to thyself, thy restless spirit ne'er Will know repose; thou tremblest at the thought Of thy son's death, yet fearest his dangerous life: Consult no more thy doubtful oracles, And hesitating priests, that brood in secret O'er the dark bosom of futurity; But hear Ægisthus, he shall give thee peace, And satisfy thy soul: this hand determines, This tongue pronounces Clytemnæstra's fate: If thou wouldst live and reign, confide in me, And me alone, and let me hear no more Of your unworthy son; but for Electra, She's to be feared, and we must think of her: Perhaps her marriage with my Plisthenes Might stop the mouth of faction, and appease The discontented people: thou wouldst wish To see the deadly hatred, that so long Hath raged between us, softened into peace; To see our interests and our hearts united: Let it be so. Go thou, and talk with her; But take good heed her pride refuses not The proffered boon, that were an insult soon She might repent of; but I hope with you, That slavery hath bowed down her haughty spirit, That this unhoped for, unexpected change From poverty and chains to rank and splendor, Joined to a mother's kind authority, And above all, to Ambition, will persuade her To seize the golden minutes, and be wise: But if she spurns the happiness that courts her, Her insolence shall meet its due reward. Your foolish fondness, and her father's name, Have fed her pride too long; but let her dread, If she submits not, a severer fate, Chains heavier far, and endless banishment.

SCENE V.

Clytemnæstra, **Electra**: **Clytemnæstra**: Come near, my daughter, and with milder looks Behold thy mother: I have mourned in secret, And wept with thee thy hard and cruel bondage, Though not unmerited; for sure thy hatred Was most unjust, Electra: as a queen, I was offended; as a mother, grieved; But I have gained your pardon, and your rights Are all restored.

Electra: O madam, at your feet—

Clytemnæstra: But I would still do more.

Electra: What more?

Clytemnæstra: Support Your race, restore the honored name of Pelops, And re-unite his long-divided children.

Electra: Ha! talkest thou of Orestes? speak, go on.

Clytemnæstra: I speak of thee, and hope at last Electra Will be Electra's friend: I know thy soul Aspires to empire, be thyself again, And let thy hopes transport thee to the throne Of Argos and Mycenæ; rise from chains And ignominious slavery to the throne Of thy great ancestors: Ægisthus yields To my entreaties, as a daughter yet He would embrace thee, to his Plisthenes Would join Electra; every hour the youth From Epidaurus is expected here; When he returns he weds you: look, my daughter, Towards the bright prospect of thy future glory, And bury all the past in deep oblivion.

Electra: Can I forget the past, or look with joy On that which is to come? O cruel fate, This is the worst indignity that e'er Electra bore: remember whence I sprang, Remember, I am Agamemnon's daughter, And wouldst thou bind me to his murderer's son? Give me my chains again, oppress my soul With all the horrors of base servitude; All that the tyrant e'er inflicted on me, Shame and reproach suit with my sad condition; I have supported them, and looked on death Without a fear: a thousand times Ægisthus Hath threatened me with death, but this is worse; Thou art more cruel far to ask my vows, My love, my honor; but I see your aim, I know your purpose; poor Orestes slain, His murderer trembles at a sister's claim, And dreads my title to a father's throne: The tyrant wants my hand to second him, To seal his poor precarious rights with mine, And make me an accomplice in his guilt: O, if I have a right Ægisthus fears, Let him erase my title in my blood, And tear it from me: if another arm Be needful to his purpose, lend him thine; Strike here, and join Electra to her brother; Strike here, and I shall know 'tis Clytemnæstra.

Clytemnæstra: It is too much: ungrateful as thou art, I pitied thee; but all my hopes are past: What have I done, what would I do, to bend Thy stubborn heart? tears, menaces, reproaches, And love and tenderness, the throne itself, Which but for me thou never couldst have hoped, Prayers, punishment, and pardon, naught availed, And now I yield thee to thy fate: farewell! Thou sayest that thou shalt know me for thy mother, For Clytemnæstra, by my cruelty: I am thy mother, and I am thy queen, Remember that; to Agamemnon's race Naught do I owe but hatred and revenge; I will not warm a serpent in my breast To sting me: henceforth storm, complain, and weep, I shall not heed the clamors of a slave: I loved thee once, with grief I own I loved thee; But from this hour remember Clytemnæstra Is not thy mother, but Ægisthus' wife; The bonds are broken that united us, Electra broke them; nature hath disclaimed, And I abjure them.

SCENE VI.

Electra: [Alone.] Gracious heaven! is this A mother's voice? O day the bitterest sure That ever rose since my dear father's death! I fear I said too much, but my full heart, Spite of myself, would pour its venom forth: She told me my Orestes was no more; Could I bear that? O if a cruel mother Has robbed me of my best, my dearest treasure, Why should I court my worst of foes, why fawn And cringe to her, to live a vile dependant On her precarious bounties; to lift up These withered hands to unrelenting heaven, To see my father's bed and throne usurped By this base spoiler, this inhuman tyrant, Who robbed me of a mother's heart, and now Hath taken Orestes from me?

SCENE VII.

Electra, Iphisa.

Iphisa: O Electra, Complain no more.

Electra: Why not?

Iphisa: Partake my joy.

Electra: Joy is a stranger to this heart, Iphisa, And ever shall be.

Iphisa: Still there is hope.

Electra: O no, Still must we weep: for if I may believe A mother, our dear brother, our Orestes, Is dead.

Iphisa: And if I may believe these eyes, He lives, he's here, Electra.

Electra: Can it be? Good heaven! O do not trifle with a heart Like mine: Iphisa, didst thou say Orestes?

Iphisa: I did.

Electra: Thou wouldst not with a flattering dream Deceive me, my Iphisa—but, go on, For hope and fear distract me.

Iphisa: O my sister, Two strangers, cast by some benignant God On these unhappy coasts, are just arrived, And hither, by the care of good Pammenes, Conducted; one of them—

Electra: I faint: die— Well, one of them—

Iphisa: I saw the noble youth: O what a lustre sparkled in his eye! His air, his mien, his every gesture bore The perfect semblage of a demi-god; Even as they paint the illustrious Grecian chief, The conqueror of Troy; such majesty And sweet deportment ne'er did I behold; But with Pammenes he retired, and hid His beauteous form from my desiring eyes: Struck with the charming image, and amazed, I ran to seek thee here, beneath the shade Of this dark grove, to tell the pleasing tale: But mark what followed—on the sacred tomb, Where we so oft have mingled our sad tears, I saw fresh garlands, saw the votive wreath, The water sprinkled over it, and the hair Doubtless of those whom I so late had seen, The illustrious strangers: near to these was laid, What most confirmed my hopes, a glittering sword, That spoke methought the day of vengeance near: Who but a son, a brother, and a hero, Raised by the gods to save his falling country, Would dare to brave the tyrant thus? 'Tis he, Electra, heaven hath sent him to our aid, The lightning glares upon us, and the thunder Will soon be heard.

Electra: I must believe Iphisa, And hope the best; but is it not a snare Laid by the tyrant? Come: we'll know the truth, Let us away—I must be satisfied.

Iphisa: We must not search him in the dark retreat Where he is hid. Pammenes says, his life Would answer for it.

Electra: Ha! what dost thou say? Alas! we are deceived, betrayed, Iphisa, By cruel heaven: thus, after fifteen years, Restored, Orestes would have run with joy

To the dear arms that saved him, would have cheered Electra's mournful heart, he ne'er had fled From thee, Iphisa: O that sword thou sawest, Which raised thy sanguine hope, alarms my fears; A cruel mother would be well informed, And in her eyes I read the barbarous joy She felt within: O dart one ray of hope, Ye vengeful gods, on my despairing soul! Will not Pammenes yield to my entreaties? He will; he must: away, I'll speak to him.

Iphisa: Do not, Electra; think what cruel eyes Watch o'er our steps, and mark our every action. If he is come, we shall discover him By our fond zeal, and hazard his sweet life: If we're deceived, our search but irritates The tyrant, and endangers good Pammenes; But let us pay our duty at the tomb, There we at least may weep without offence. Who knows, Electra, but the noble stranger May meet us in that blest asylum; there That heaven, whose goodness thy impatient rage Hath called in question, may yet hear my vows, And give him to our wishes and our tears: Let us be gone.

Electra: Thou hast revived my hopes: But O, I die with grief, if thou deceivest me!

ACT III.

SCENE I.

Orestes, Pylades, Pammenes [A slave at the farther end of the stage carrying an urn and a sword.]

Pammenes: Blest be the day that to our wishes thus Restores the long-expected hope of Greece, My royal master's son, the minister Of heaven's high will, to execute swift vengeance On Agamemnon's foes! The tyrant long Hath dreaded, long foreseen the impending blow; Conscious of guilt, in every face unknown Still he beholds his master and his judge, And still Orestes haunts his troubled soul: Much he inquires concerning you, and longs To see you both. I have a thousand fears, A thousand hopes; heaven grant we may succeed! Meantime I have obeyed your orders, sounded The people's hearts, and strove to animate Their zeal; inspired them with the distant hope Of an avenger; soon or late the race Of rightful kings must prosper: every heart Glowed with warm transport at Orestes' name; Awakened from her slumber, vengeance rises With double vigor; my few faithful friends, Who dwell in this lone desert with Pammenes, Lift up their hands to heaven, and call on thee; And yet I tremble to behold thee here Unarmed and unassisted, lest some chance Discover thee, and blast our hopes: the foe Is barbarous, active, vigilant, and bold; One fatal stroke may ruin all; whilst thou, Against a tyrant seated on his throne, Bringest nothing but Orestes, and his friend.

Pylades: And are not they sufficient? 'Tis the work Of heaven that oft fulfils its own designs By means most wonderful, that in the deep O'erwhelmed our little all, and here alone Hath left us to perform the sacrifice. Sometimes it arms the sovereigns of the earth With tenfold vengeance; sometimes, in contempt Of human valor, strikes in awful silence; Nature and friendship then assert the rights Of heaven, and vindicate its power divine.

Orestes: Orestes asks no other aid, no arm But thine, my Pylades.

Pylades: Take heed, my friend, Quit not the paths of safety pointed out By the just gods; remember thou art bound By solemn oath to hide thee from Electra;

Thy peace, thy happiness, thy kingdom, all Depend upon it: O refrain thy transports, Dissemble, and obey; 'tis fit Electra Should be deceived, even more than Clytemnæstra.

Pammenes: Thank heaven, that thus ordained it for thy safety. Already hath Electra, bathed in tears, And calling for her great avenger, filled These solitary mansions with her cries; Importunate and bold, she sought me out, And with imprudent warmth, demanded loud, Where was her brother, where her dear Orestes: Nature had whispered to her anxious heart He was not far from his Electra: scarce Could I withhold her eager steps.

Orestes: Ye gods! Must I refrain? O insupportable!

Pylades: You hesitate; O think, my dear Orestes, Think on the menaces of angry heaven, Think on its goodness that preserved thy life From every danger; if thou shouldst oppose Its sacred will, eternal wrath awaits To blast thy purpose; tremble, son of Atreus And Tantalus, remember what thy hapless race Hath suffered, nor expect a milder doom.

Orestes: What power invincible presides unseen O'er human actions, and directs our fate? Is it a crime to listen to the voice Of fond affection? O eternal justice, Thou deep abyss, unsearchable to man! Shall not our weakness and our guilt by thee Be still distinguished? shall the man who wanders From virtue's paths unknowing, and who braves Thy power, shall he who yields to nature's laws, And he who breaks them, share an equal fate? But shall the slave condemn his master? heaven Gave us our being, and can owe us nothing: Therefore no more: in silence I obey. Give me the urn, the ring, and bloody sword, Which thou hast hither brought, they shall be offered Far from Electra's sight: let us be gone; I'll see my sister when I have avenged her. [Turning to Pammenes.] Go thou, Pammenes, and prepare the hearts Of thy brave followers for the great event Which Greece awaits, and I must execute: Deceive Ægisthus, and my guilty mother; Let them enjoy the transitory bliss, The short-lived pleasure of Orestes' death, If an unnatural mother can behold With joy the ashes of a murdered son: Here will I wait, and stop them as they pass.

SCENE II.

Electra and Iphisa on one side of the stage Orestes and Pylades on the other, with a slave carrying an urn and a sword.

Electra: [To Iphisa.] Hope disappointed is the worst of sorrows. O my Iphisa, all thy flattering dreams Are vanished, and Pammenes, with a word, Hath undeceived us; the fair day that shone So bright is clouded o'er, and darkness spreads On every side: alas! our wretched life Is but a round of never-ending woes.

Orestes: [To Pylades.] Two women, and in tears!

Pylades: Alas, my lord, Beneath a tyrant all things wear the face Of grief and misery.

Orestes: In Ægisthus' court Nothing should reign but sorrow.

Iphisa: [To Electra.] Look, Electra, The strangers come this way.

Electra: Unhappy omen! They did pronounce Ægisthus' hated name.

Iphisa: One is that hero whom I told thee of, The noble youth—

Electra: [Looking at Orestes.] Alas! I too, like thee, Have been deceived. [Turning to Orestes.] Who are ye, wretched strangers; And what hath led you to this fatal shore?

Orestes: We come to see the king who reigns in Argos, And take our orders from him.

Electra: Are ye Grecians, And call ye him a king, the murderer Of Agamemnon?

Orestes: He is sovereign here, And heaven commands us to respect his throne, Not to dispute his title.

Electra: Horrid maxim! And what have you to ask of this proud king, This bloody monster here?

Orestes: We come to bring him Some happy tidings.

Electra: Dreadful then to us They must be.

Iphisa: [Seeing the Urn.] Ha! an urn! O grief, O horror!

Pylades: Orestes—

Electra: O ye gods! Orestes dead! I faint, I die.

Orestes: What have we done, my friend! They could not be mistaken, for their grief Betrays them: O! my blood runs cold.—Fair princess, Be comforted, and live.

Electra: Orestes dead? And can I live? O no, barbarians, here Complete your cruelty.

Iphisa: Alas! you see The poor remains of Agamemnon; we Are his unhappy daughters, the sad sisters Of lost Orestes.

Orestes: O Electra! O Iphisa! O where am I? cruel gods! [To the slave carrying the urn.] Take from their sight those monuments of woe, That fatal urn, which—

Electra: [Running towards the urn.] Wouldst thou take it from me? Wouldst thou deprive me of the little all That's left Electra by offended heaven? O give it me. [She takes the urn, and embraces it.]

Orestes: Forbear; what wouldst thou do?

Pylades: Away: Ægisthus only must receive These precious relics.

Electra: Must I then behold My brother's ashes in a tyrant's hand, And are Orestes' murderers before me?

Orestes: Horrid reproach! it shocks my very soul: I can no longer—

Electra: Yet you weep with me: O, in the name of the avenging gods, If ye are guiltless, if your generous hands Collected his dear ashes—

Orestes: Gracious heaven!

Electra: If ye lament his death, O answer me: Who told you of his fate: art thou his friend? Speak, noble youth: both dumb! yet both afflicted: Even whilst your words plant daggers in my heart, Ye seem to pity me.

Orestes: It is too much; The gods have been obeyed enough already.

Electra: What sayest thou?

Orestes: Leave those poor remains.

Electra: O no: I never will: alas! is every heart Inflexible? I tell thee, cruel stranger, I must not, cannot give thee back again The fatal gift thy pity hath bestowed: 'Tis my Orestes; and I will embrace him: Behold his dying sister.

Orestes: Cruel gods! Where are your thunders now? O strike: Electra, I can no longer—

Electra: Ha!

Orestes: I ought—

Pylades: O heaven!

Electra: Go on—

Orestes: Know then—

SCENE III.

Ægisthus, Clytemnæstra, Orestes, Pylades, Electra, Iphisa, Pammenes, Guards.

Ægisthus: O glorious spectacle! Fortune, I thank thee: Can it be, Pammenes? My rival dead! it is, it must be true, Electra's grief confirms it.

Electra: Dreadful hour?

Orestes: To what am I reserved?

Ægisthus: Seize on the urn, And wrest it from her. [They take the urn from her.]

Electra: O thou hast robbed me of the only good This life could e'er afford me, barbarous monster! O take Electra too, tear forth this heart And join me to Orestes; father, son, Sister, and brother, all thy wretched victims Unite to satiate thy revenge: now, tyrant, Enjoy thy happiness, enjoy thy crimes: And thou, inhuman mother, look with him On the delightful spectacle, it suits Thy nature, and is worthy of you both. [Iphisa leads her off.]

SCENE IV.

ægisthus, clytemnæstra, orestes, pylades, Guards. **Clytemnæstra:** Must I bear this?

Ægisthus: She shall be punished for it: Let her complain to heaven, for heaven itself Will justify Ægisthus; it approves Where it forbids not; therefore I am guiltless, And happy too: my throne stands firmly now, My life's in safety; but I must reward The zeal and valor of these noble Grecians.

Orestes: It was our duty, royal sir, to lay These proofs before you: take this sword, this ring, You must remember it: 'twas Agamemnon's.

Clytemnæstra: And was it then by thee Orestes fell?

Ægisthus: If thou hast served me, thine be the reward: But, say, who art thou, of what race?

Orestes: My name Must not as yet be known; perhaps hereafter It may be: in the fields of Troy my father Distinguished shone amongst the great avengers Of Menelaus; in those days of glory He fought, and fell: deserted and forlorn, Left by a cruel mother, and pursued By most inhuman foes, this friend alone Supported me; was fortune, father, all; With him I still have trod the paths of honor, With him defied the malice of my fate: Such is my story.

Ægisthus: But say where thy arm Avenged me of this hated prince: inform me.

Orestes: 'Twas a word that to the temple leads Of Epidaurus, near Achemor's tomb.

Ægisthus: The king had set a price upon his head: How came you not to ask for your reward?

Orestes: Because I hated infamy, and fought For vengeance, not for hire; I did not mean To sell his blood; a private motive raised This arm against him, as my friend well knows, And I revenged myself without the aid Of kings, nor shall I boast the victory: Forgive me, sir: I tremble; for the widow Of Agamemnon's here; perhaps I've served, Perhaps offended her; I'll take my leave.

Ægisthus: Thou shalt not; stay, I charge thee.

Clytemnæstra: Let him go: That urn, and the sad story he has told, Have filled my soul with horror: heaven, my lord, Protects your throne and life, be thankful for it, And leave a mother to indulge her sorrows.

Orestes: Madam, I thought that Agamemnon's son Was hateful to you.

Clytemnæstra: I must own I feared him.

Orestes: Feared him?

Clytemnæstra: I did indeed; for he was born To be most guilty.

Orestes: Guilty? and to whom?

Clytemnæstra: The wretched wanderer, thou knowest, was doomed To hate a mother, doomed to shed the blood From whence he sprang; such was his horrid fate: Perhaps he had fulfilled—and yet, his death, I know not why, affrights me, and I tremble To look on you who saved me from his vengeance.

Orestes: Alas! a son against a mother armed! O who could loose that sacred tie? perhaps He wished—

Clytemnæstra: O heaven!

Ægisthus: What sayest thou? didst thou know him?

Pylades: [Aside.] He will discover all. [To Ægisthus.] He did, my lord, The wretched soon unite, and soon divide: At Delphi first we saw him.

Orestes: Yes: I know His purpose well.

Ægisthus: What was it?

Orestes: To murder thee.

Ægisthus: I've seen his malice long, but I despised it. Meantime Electra used Orestes' name To spread division o'er my kingdom; she Was my worst foe: thou hast avenged me of her, Take thy reward, I yield her to thy power; She shall be thine: the haughty maid, who spurned The great alliance with Ægisthus' son; Henceforth she is thy slave: the wretched race Of Priam long beneath the conqueror's yoke Submissive bowed, and dragged the servile chain; And wherefore should not Agememnon's blood Bend in its turn, and share an equal fate?

Clytemnæstra: Would Clytemnæstra suffer that!

Ægisthus: Thou wouldst not Defend thy worst of foes; proscribe Orestes, Yet spare Electra. [To Orestes.] Leave the urn with me.

Orestes: We will, my lord, and shall accept your offer.

Clytemnæstra: That were to carry our resentment further Than justice warrants: let him hence, and bear Some other recompense: we too must go: Let us, my lord, I beg thee, let us quit These horrid mansions of the dead, where naught But dreadful images on every side Surrounds me: O we never can prepare The bloody feast between the father's tomb And the son's ashes! How shall we invoke The household gods, whom we have injured; how, Amidst our cruel sports, give up the blood Of Clytemnæstra to the murderer Of her Orestes? O it must not be! I tremble at the thought: my fears, Ægisthus, Should waken thine: this stranger rives my heart; His very sight is deadliest poison to me. Away, my lord, and let me be concealed From every eye; would it were possible To hide me from myself! [Exit Clytemnæstra]

Ægisthus: [To Orestes.] Stay thou, and wait Till time befriend thee; nature for a moment Is clamorous and loud, but soon as reason Shall reassume its empire, interest then Must plead thy cause, and she alone be heard. Meantime remain with us, and celebrate Our nuptial day: [To one of his attendants.] Haste you to Epidaurus, And hither bring my son; let him confirm The welcome tidings.

SCENE V.

Orestes, Pylades.

Orestes: Yes, Orestes comes To join the cruel pomp, and make thy feast A feast of blood.

Pylades: O how I trembled for thee! I feared thy love; I feared thy tenderness; And, more than all, thy honest rage, that burst In transports forth when thou beheldest the tyrant: I saw thee ready to insult him; saw Thy soul take fire at Agamemnon's name, And dreaded the sad consequence.

Orestes: My mother, O, Pylades, my mother pierced my heart. Didst thou not mark the workings of her soul Whilst I was speaking? O I felt them all! Scarce could my voice in faltering accents tell The melancholy tale, whilst Clytemnæstra Still gazed, and trembled still: a father's murder; A sister unrevenged; a tyrant yet Unpunished; and a mother to be taught Her interest and her duty; what a weight Of secret cares! great heaven complete thy work! Urge on the lingering moments that retard My vengeance; O, let me perform the task Of love, and hatred; let me mix the blood Of base Ægisthus with the vile remains Of Plisthenes; let sweet Electra see The cruel tyrant gasping at my feet, And know her dear deliverer in Orestes!

SCENE VI.

Orestes, Pylades, Pammenes.

Orestes: What hast thou done, Pammenes, may we hope—

Pammenes: O my dear lord, never, since the fatal day When Agamemnon fell, did greater perils Threaten thy precious life.

Orestes: Ha! what hath happened?

Pylades: Still Must I have cause to tremble for Orestes?

Pammenes: This instant is arrived a messenger From Epidaurus, and ere this related The death of Plisthenes.

Pylades: Immortal gods!

Orestes: And knows he that Orestes slew his son?

Pammenes: They speak of nothing but his death; ere long Fresh tidings are expected; and the news Meantime concealed from Greece that she has lost One of her tyrants; the king, still in doubt, Shuts himself up with Clytemnæstra: this I learned from one, who, to the royal blood Still faithful, pines in loathsome servitude Beneath the proud usurper.

Orestes: I have gathered At least the first fair fruits of promised vengeance; Grant me, ye gods, to reap a plenteous harvest! Thinkest thou, my friend, they would uplift this arm In vain, and only prosper to deceive me; To my successful valor give the son, And after yield me to the father's power? Let us away: danger should make us bold; Who fears not death is master of his foe; I'll seize the moment of uncertainty, Ere the full day of truth glares in upon him, And points his rage.

Pammenes: Away: you must be known To those few noble spirits who will die To serve their prince; this secret place conceals Some faithful friends, who may be still more useful, Because unknown.

Pylades: Haste then; and if the tomb Of thy dear father, if thy honored name Joined to Electra's, if the wrath of heaven Against usurpers, if the gracious gods Who hither led thee, if they all should fail, If this detested spot is doomed by fate To be thy grave, O take a wretched life To thee devoted, we will die together, That comfort's left; for Pylades shall fall Close by thy side, and worthy of Orestes.

Orestes: Strike me, kind heaven! but O for pity save His matchless valor, and protect my friend!

ACT IV.

SCENE I.

Orestes, Pylades.

Orestes: Perhaps the vigilance of good Pammenes May for awhile remove the king's suspicions; And gracious heaven, in pity to our woes, Deceive Ægisthus to a fond belief, That the devoted race of Tantalus Is now no more; but, O my Pylades, The sword I offered at my father's tomb Is stolen by sacrilegious hands, that reach Even to the sacred mansions of the dead: If it be carried to the tyrant, all Will be discovered; let us haste, my friend, And seize him, ere it be too late.

Pylades: Pammenes Is watchful o'er our interest: we must wait For him: when we have gathered the few friends That mean to serve us, be this tomb the place Of meeting for us all, Pammenes then Will join us here.

Orestes: O Pylades, O heaven! This barbarous law that forces me to wound A tender heart that lives but for Orestes! And must I leave Electra to her sorrows?

Pylades: Yes: thou hast sworn it, therefore persevere; Thou hast more cause to dread Electra now Than all thy foes; she may destroy, but never Can serve us, and the tyrant's eyes may soon Be opened: O subdue, if possible, The pangs of nature, and conceal thy love: We came not here to comfort thy Electra, But to avenge her.

Orestes: See, my Pylades, She comes this way, perhaps in search of me.

Pylades: Her every step is watched: you must not see her: Begone; and doubt not, I'll observe her well; The eyes of friendship seldom are deceived.

SCENE II.

Electra, Iphisa, Pylades.

Electra: The villain hath escaped me; he avoids My hated sight, and leaves me to my fate, To fruitless rage, and unavailing tears, Without the hope of vengeance: say, barbarian, Thou vile accomplice in his crimes, where went The murderer, my tyrant, my new lord, (For so it seems Ægisthus has decreed) Where is he gone?

Pylades: To do the will of heaven, In dutiful obedience to the gods, And well would it become the royal maid To follow his example: fate ofttimes Deceives the hearts of men, directs in secret, And guides their wandering steps through paths unknown; Ofttimes it sinks us in the deep abyss Of misery, and then raises us to joy; Binds us in chains, or lifts us to a throne, And gives us life midst horrors, tombs, and death. Complain no more, but yield to thy new sorrows; Be patient, and be happy: fare thee well.

SCENE III.

Electra, Iphisa.

Electra: He swells my rage to fury and despair: Thinks he I'll tamely bear these cruel insults? Could not a father's and a brother's death Fill up the measure of Electra's woes; But she must bend beneath the vile assassin Of her Orestes; be a common slave To all the murderers of her hapless race? Thou dreadful sword, wet with Orestes' blood, Exposed in triumph at the sacred tomb, Thou execrable trophy, for a moment Thou didst deceive me, but thou hast insulted The ashes of the dead; I'll make thee serve A nobler purpose: though Ægisthus hides His guilty head, and with the queen in secret Plans future crimes, and meditates destruction, Still we may find the murderer of Orestes: I cannot bathe me in the blood of both My tyrants, but on one at least my soul Shall be revenged.

Iphisa: I cannot blame the grief Which I partake; but hear me, hear the voice Of reason; every tongue speaks of Orestes; They say, he lives, and the king's fears confirm it. You saw Pammenes talking with this stranger In secret, saw his ardent zeal to serve And to attend him: thinkest thou, our best friend, Our comforter, the good old man, would e'er Associate with a murderer? never, never, He could not be so base.

Electra: He may be false, Or weak; old age is easily deceived: We are betrayed by all; I know we are: Did not the cruel stranger boast his deed? Did not

Ægisthus yield me up a victim? Was not Electra made the price of guilt, The murderer's reward? Orestes calls me To join him in the tomb: now then, my sister, If e'er thou lovest Electra, pity her In her last moments; bloody they must be, And terrible. Away; inform thyself Touching Pammenes; see if the assassin Be with the queen: she flatters all my foes; She heard unmoved the murder of her son, And seemed, O gods! a mother seemed, to share The guilty transport with her savage lord. O that this sword could reach him in her arms, And pierce the traitor's heart! I'll do it.

Iphisa: No more: Indeed you wrong her; for the sight of him Offends her: be not thus precipitate And rash, Electra; I will to Pammenes, And talk with him: or I am much deceived, Or by their silence they but mean to hide Some mystery from us: your imprudent warmth (Yet who would not forgive it in the wretched?) Perhaps alarms them, and they would conceal From you their purpose; what it is, I know not: Pammenes seems to shun you, let me go And speak to him; but do not, my Electra, Hazard a deed thou wilt too late repent of.

SCENE IV.

Electra: The subtle tyrants have gained o'er Pammenes; Old age is weak and fearful: what can faith Or friendship do against the hand of power? Henceforth Electra to herself alone Shall trust her vengeance: 'tis enough: these hands, Armed with despair, shall act with double vigor. Arise ye furies, leave your dark abode For seats more guilty, and another hell, Open your dreary caverns, and receive Your victims: bring your flaming torches here, Daughters of vengeance, arm yourselves and me; Approach, with death and terror in your train; Orestes, Agamemnon, and Electra Invoke your aid: and lo! they come, I see Their glittering swords, and unappalled behold them; They are not half so dreadful as Ægisthus: The murderer comes; and see, they throng around him; Hell points him out, and yields him to my vengeance.

SCENE V.

Electra: [At the bottom of the stage.]

Orestes: [On the other side at a distance from her.] Where am I? hither they directed me: O my dear country! and thou, fatal spot That gave me birth, thou great but guilty race Of Tantalus, for ever shall thy blood Be wretched? horror here on every side Surrounds me: wherefore am I punished thus? What have I done? why must Orestes suffer For his forefathers' crimes?

Electra: [Advancing a little from the bottom of the stage.] What power withholds me? I cannot lift my arm against him; but I will go on.

Orestes: Methought I heard a voice: O my dear father, ever-honored shade, Much injured Agamemnon, didst thou groan?

Electra: Just heaven! durst he pronounce that sacred name? And see he weeps: can sighs and penitence Find entrance here? but what is his remorse To the dire horrors that Electra feels! [She comes forward.] He is alone; now strike—die, traitor—O I cannot—

Orestes: Gods! Electra, art thou here, Furious and trembling?

Electra: Sure thou art some god Who thus unnervest me—thou has slain my brother: I would have taken thy life for it, but the sword Dropped from my hand; thy genius hath prevailed; I yield to thee, and must betray my brother.

Orestes: Betray him, no! O, why am I restrained?—

Electra: At sight of thee my resolution dies, And all is changed: could it be thou who filled My soul with terror?

Orestes: O, I would repay Thy precious tears with hazard of my life!

Electra: Methought I heard thee speak of Agamemnon. O gentle youth, deceive me not, but speak: For I had well nigh done a desperate deed; O show me all the guilt of it! explain The mystery; tell me who thou art.

Orestes: O sister Of dear Orestes, fly from me, avoid me.

Electra: But wherefore? speak.

Orestes: No more—I am—take heed They see us not together.

Electra: Gracious heaven! Thou fillest my heart with terror and with joy.

Orestes: O if thou lovest thy brother—

Electra: Love him! yes: And O in thee I hear a father's voice, And see his features; nature hath unveiled The mystery: O be kind and speak for her, Do not deny it; say thou art my brother: Thou art, I know thou art—my dear Orestes; How could a sister seek thy precious life?

Orestes: [Embracing her.] Heaven threatens in vain, and nature will prevail: Electra is more powerful than the gods.

Electra: The gods have given a sister to thy vows, And dost thou fear their wrath?

Orestes: Their cruel orders Would have deprived me of my dear Electra, And may perhaps chastise a brother's weakness.

Electra: Thy weakness there was virtue; O rejoice With me, Orestes; wherefore wouldst thou force me To that rash act? it might have cost thee dear.

Orestes: I've broken my sacred promise.

Electra: 'Twas thy duty.

Orestes: A secret trusted to me by the gods.

Electra: I drew it from thee; I extorted it; Mine be the guilt; an oath more sacred far Binds me to vengeance: what hast thou to fear?

Orestes: My destiny, the oracles, the blood From whence I sprung.

Electra: That blood henceforth shall flow In purer streams; haste then, and join with me To scourge the guilty; oracles and gods Are all propitious to our great design, And the same power that saved will guide Orestes.

SCENE VI.

electra, orestes, pylades, pammenes. **Electra**: Rejoice with me, my friends, for I have found My dear Orestes.

Pylades: [To Orestes.] Hast thou then revealed The dangerous secret? Couldst thou think—

Orestes: If heaven Expects obedience, it must give us laws We can obey.

Electra: Canst thou reproach him thus Only for making poor Electra happy? Wouldst thou adopt the cruel sentiments Of persecuting foes, and hide Orestes From my embraces? what unjust decree What harsh commands—

Pylades: I meant to save him for thee, That he might live, and be thy great avenger.

Pammenes: Princess, thou knowest, in this detested place They watch thee nearly; every sigh is heard, And every motion carefully observed: Those private friends, whose humble state eludes The tyrants search, adore this noble youth, And would have served him; everything's prepared; But thy imprudence now will hazard all.

Electra: Did not Ægisthus give me to a hand, Stained, as he thought, with my Orestes' blood? [To Orestes.] Thou art my master; I am bound to serve thee; I will obey the tyrant; his commands, For once, are welcome, and the prospect brightens On every side.

Pammenes: It may be clouded soon, Ægisthus is alarmed, and we have cause To tremble; if he but suspects us, death Must be our portion, therefore let us part.

Pylades: [To Pammenes.] Hence, good Pammenes, bring our friends together, The hours are precious; haste and finish soon Thy noble work; 'tis time we should appear, And—like ourselves.

SCENE VII.

ægisthus, clytemnæstra, electra, orestes, pylades, Guards. **Ægisthus**: Slaves, execute your office, And bear these traitors to the dungeon.

Orestes: Once There ruled o'er Argos those who better knew The rights of hospitality.

Pylades: Ægisthus, What is our crime? Inform us, and at least Respect this noble youth.

Ægisthus: Away with them; Ye stand aghast, as if ye feared to touch His sacred person: hence, I say, take heed Ye disobey me not: guards, drag them off.

Electra: O stay, barbarian, stay; for heaven itself Pleads for their sacred lives—they tear them from me, O gods!

Ægisthus: Electra, tremble for thyself, Perfidious as thou art, and dread my wrath.

SCENE VIII.

Electra, Clytemnæstra.

Electra: O hear me, if thou art a mother, hear; Let me recall thy former tenderness, Forgive my guilty rage, the sad effect Of unexampled sorrows; to complain, Is still, the mournful privilege of grief: Pity these wretched strangers; heaven perhaps, Whose dreadful vengeance thou so long hast feared, May for their sakes forgive thy past offences; The pardon thou bestowest on them may plead For thee: O save them, save them.

Clytemnæstra: Why shouldst thou Be thus solicitous? What interest prompts Thy ardent zeal?

Electra: Thou seest, the gods protect them, Who saved them from the Ocean's boisterous rage, And brought them here: heaven gives them to thy care, And will require them at thy hands—to one, O if thou knewest him—but they both are wretched. Are we in Argos, or at Tauris, where The cruel priestess bids her altars smoke With stranger's blood? What must I do to save him?

Command, and I obey: to Plisthenes You'd have me wedded; I submit, though death Were far more welcome; lead me to his bed.

Clytemnæstra: You mean to mock us: knowest thou not, he's dead?

Electra: Just heaven! and hath Ægisthus lost a son?

Clytemnæstra: I see the joy that sparkles in thy eyes; Thou art pleased to hear it.

Electra: No: I am too wretched To be delighted with another's woe: I pity the unhappy, nor would shed The blood of innocence: O save the strangers! I ask no more.

Clytemnæstra: Away: I understand thee, And know thee but too well; thou hast confirmed The king's suspicions, and revealed the secret: One of these strangers is—Orestes.

Electra: Well, Suppose it were; suppose that gracious heaven, In tender pity, had restored thy son—

Clytemnæstra: O dreadful moment! how am I to act?

Electra: Is it a doubt, and canst thou hesitate? Thy son! O heaven! think on his past misfortunes, Think on his merits; but if still thy mind Is doubtful, all is lost: farewell Orestes.

Clytemnæstra: I'm not in doubt; I am resolved; even thou, With all thy fury, canst not change the love, The tenderness I bear him: I will guard, Save, and protect him—he may punish me, Perhaps he will; I tremble at his name; No matter—I'm a mother still, and love My children; thou mayst yet preserve thy hate.

Electra: No: I will fall submissive at thy feet, And thank thy bounty: now, indulgent heaven, Thy mercy shines superior to thy wrath; For thou hast given a mother to my vows, Changed her resentful heart, and saved Orestes.

ACT V.

SCENE I.

Electra: I am forbid to enter here; oppressed With fears, in vain I lift these hands to heaven: Iphisa comes not; but behold the gates Are opened: ha! she's here, I tremble.

SCENE II.

Electra, Iphisa.

Electra: Say, My dear Iphisa, what have I to hope, Will Clytemnæstra dare to be a mother? Has she the power, has she the will to make us Some poor amends for all the cruel evils She has inflicted on us? Could she e'er— But she's a slave to guilt, and to Ægisthus: I am prepared to hear the worst; O speak, Say, all is past, and we must die.

Iphisa: I hope, And yet I fear: Ægisthus hath received Some dark suggestions, but is doubtful still, Whether Orestes is his prisoner here, And Clytemnæstra never named her son: She seems to feel a mother's fondness for him, And, pierced with anguish, trembles for his life: She struggles with herself, and fears alike To speak or to be silent; strives to soothe The tyrant's rage, and save them from his vengeance: But should Orestes once be known, he dies.

Electra: O cruel thought! perhaps when I implored My barbarous mother I destroyed Orestes; Her grief will but enrage the fierce Ægisthus; Nature is ever fatal here: I dread Her silence, and yet would not have her speak; Danger is on every side: but say, Iphisa, What hath Pammenes done?

Iphisa: His feeble age Seems strengthened by misfortune, and our dangers But breathe new spirit o'er his ardent zeal To serve our cause; he animates our friends With double vigor; even the servile throng, That cringe around the tyrant's throne, begin To murmur at the name of great Orestes: Veterans, who served beneath the father, burn With honest ardor to support the son: Such power have justice and the sacred laws O'er mortal minds, howe'er by vice corrupted.

Electra: O that Electra could inflame their souls With glowing virtue, breathe her own fierce spirit Into their timid hearts, and animate Their cold resentment! would I had but known, Ere he arrived on this detested shore, That my Orestes lived! or that Pammenes Had further urged—

SCENE III.

Ægisthus, Clytemnæstra, Electra, Iphisa, Guards.

Ægisthus: Guards, seize that hoary traitor, And let him be confronted with those strangers Whom I have doomed to death; he is their friend, And confidant, the accomplice in their crimes: How dreadful was the snare which they had laid! O, Claytemnæstra, 'tis the cursed Orestes, It must be he; do not deceive thyself, Do not defend him: O, I see it all, It is too plain: alas! this urn contains The ashes of my son: the murderers brought This fatal present to his weeping father.

Clytemnæstra: Canst thou believe—

Ægisthus: I can; I must rely On the sworn hatred 'twixt the unhappy children Of Atreus and Thyestes; must believe The time, the place, the rage of fierce Electra, Iphisa's tears, your undeserved compassion, Your ill-timed pity for these base assassins; Orestes lives, and I have lost my son; But I have caught him in the toils; whiche'er It be, for yet I know not, I'll be just, I'll sacrifice the murderer to my son, And to his mother.

Clytemnæstra: Horrid sacrifice! I must not see it.

Ægisthus: Horrible to thee?

Clytemnæstra: O yes; already blood enough hath flowed In this sad scene of slaughter: O 'tis time To end the woes of Pelops' hapless race: If after all it should not be Orestes, Wouldst thou, on dark suspicion's vague report, Murder the innocent? and if it be Indeed my son, my lord, I must defend him, Must gain his pardon at thy hands, or perish.

Ægisthus: I cannot, dare not yield to thy request; For thy own sake I dare not; thy fond pity May be thy ruin; all that melts thy heart To soft compassion, sharpens mine to rage And fierce resentment: one of them I know Must be Orestes, therefore both shall die; I ought not even to hesitate a moment: Guards, do your office.

Iphisa: O, my lord, behold me Low at your feet; must all our hapless race Thus humbly bend, thus supplicate in vain? Electra, kneel with me, embrace his knees, Thy pride destroys us.

Electra: Can I stoop so low? Shall I bring foul disgrace on thee, my brother, And ignominy, and shame? it shocks my soul; But I will suffer all to save Orestes. [Turning to Ægisthus.] It thou wilt save him, here I promise thee, (Not to forget my father's murder, that I never can, but) in respectful silence To pay thee homage, still to live with thee A willing slave, let but my brother live.

Ægisthus: Thy brother dies, and thou shalt live a slave; My vengeance is complete: thy pride is humbled, And sues in vain.

Clytemnæstra: Ægisthus, 'tis too much, To trample thus on the unhappy race Of him who was thy master once; away, Spite of thy rage, I will defend my son; Deaf as thou art to a fond sister's prayers, A mother's may prevail: O think, my lord, Think on thy happy state, above the reach Of adverse fortune no, Orestes ne'er Can hurt thee, and Electra bends submissive Beneath thy power, Iphisa at thy feet; Can nothing move thee? I have gone too far Already with thee in the paths of guilt, And offered up a dreadful sacrifice. Thinkest thou I'll yield thee up my purest blood To glut thy rage? Am I forever doomed To take a murderous husband to my arms? At Aulis one a lovely daughter slew, The other threatens to destroy my son Before my eyes, close to his father's tomb: O rather let this fatal diadem, Hateful to Greece, and to myself a load Of misery, fall with me, and be no more Remembered! O Ægisthus, well thou knowest, I loved thee, 'tis amongst my blackest crimes, And stands the foremost; but I love my children, And will defend them; against thy arm upraised To shed their blood will lift my vengeful hand, And blast thy purpose: tremble, for thou knowest me: The bands are sacred that united us, Thy interest is most dear to Clytemnæstra: Remember still, Orestes is my son, And fear his mother.

Electra: You surpass my hopes. Surely a heart like thine could ne'er be guilty; Go on, my honored mother, and avenge Your children, and your husband.

Ægisthus: Slave, thou fillest The measure of thy crimes: gods! shall Ægisthus Withhold his vengeance for a woman's cries, For Agamemnon's widow, and her children? Unhappy queen! say, whom dost thou accuse? Whom dost thou plead for? hear me and obey. Away with them to instant death.

SCENE IV.

Ægisthus, Clytemnæstra, Electra, Iphisa, Dymas.

Dymas: My lord?

Ægisthus: Thou seemest disordered: what has happened? Speak.

Dymas: Orestes is discovered.

Iphisa: Ha! where is he?

Clytemnæstra: My son!

Electra: My brother?

Ægisthus: Have you punished him As he deserves?

Dymas: My lord, as yet he lives.

Ægisthus: And wherefore were my orders disobeyed?

Dymas: His friend and fellow-captive, Pylades, Pointed him out, and to the soldiers showed Great Agamemnon's son; they seemed much moved; I dread the consequence.

Ægisthus: I must prevent it, For they shall die: who dares not to revenge me Shall feel my justice: Dymas, follow me: Stay thou and guard his sisters; I defy The blood of Agamemnon: from the father Of Plisthenes, and great Thyestes' son, What mortal, or what god, shall save Orestes?

SCENE V.

clytemnæstra, electra, iphisa. **Iphisa:** Fear not, but follow him; Electra, speak, Exhort our friends, and animate their zeal.

Electra: [To Clytemnæstra.] O, in the name of powerful nature, now Complete thy noble work; conduct us, fly—

Clytemnæstra: You must not hence, the guards will not permit it: Stay here, my children, and rely on me, On a fond mother, and a tender wife: I will perform the double task, and take Orestes and Ægisthus to my care.

SCENE VI.

Electra, Iphisa.

Iphisa: Alas! the avenging god pursues us still; Though she defends Orestes, still Ægisthus Is at her heart; perhaps the tender cries Of pity and remorse shall naught avail Against the tyrant; he is proud, revengeful, Implacable, and furious; who shall save If he condemns? we must submit, and die.

Electra: O that before my death I had not fallen So low as to entreat him, to belie My honest heart, and supplicate the tyrant! Despair and horror sink me to the tomb With infamy and shame; my vain endeavors To save Orestes but urge on his fate. Where are these boasted friends Pammenes talked of, Who, with fell rancor, and determined hate, Pursued Ægisthus? Where those vengeful gods Who hid Orestes from my sight, upraised His righteous arm, and promised to support him? Where are ye now, infernal goddesses, Daughters of night, ye who so lately shook Your dreadful torches here? all nature once United seemed to guard and to protect us, But all desert us now, all court Ægisthus, And men and gods, and heaven and hell betray me.

SCENE VII.

Electra, Pylades, Iphisa.

Electra: What sayest thou, Pylades? the deed is done?

Pylades: It is: Electra's free, and heaven obeyed.

Electra: How?

Pylades: Yes, Orestes reigns: he sent me hither.

Iphisa: Just gods!

Electra: Orestes! is it possible! I faint, I die with joy.

Pylades: Orestes lives, And has avenged the blood of innocence.

Electra: What wondrous power hath wrought this strange event.

Pylades: His father's name, Electra's, and his own; His valor, and his virtue; our misfortunes, Justice, and pity; and the power that pleads In human hearts for wretchedness like thine. Pammenes, by the tyrant's order bound, Was led with us to death; in weeping crowds The people followed, and deplored our fate: I saw their rage was equal to their fears, But the guards watched them closely: then Orestes Cried, "Strike, ye slaves, and sacrifice the last Of Argos' kings; ye dare not." When he spoke, On his fair front such native majesty And royal lustre shone, we almost thought Great Agamemnon's spirit from the tomb Had risen, and came once more to bless mankind. I spoke, and friendship's happy voice prevailed; The people rose, the soldiers stood aghast, And dropped the uplifted falchions from their hands; The crowd encircled us, and desperate love, With friendship joined, fought nobly for Orestes; The joyful people bore him off in triumph: Ægisthus flew to seize his destined prey, And in the slave he meant to punish, found A conqueror: pleased I saw his humbled pride; His friends deserted, and his guards betrayed him: The insulting people triumphed in his fall. O glorious day! O all discerning justice! Ægisthus wears the chains that bound Orestes; The queen alone attends, protects, and saves him From the mad crowd, that press tumultuous on, Big with revenge, and thirsting for his blood; While Clytemnæstra holds him in her arms, And shields him from their rage, implores Orestes To save her husband: he respects her still, Fulfils the duties of a son and brother: Safe from the foe you will behold him soon Triumphant here, a conqueror and a king.

Iphisa: Let us away, to greet the loved Orestes, And comfort our afflicted mother.

Electra: Gods! What unexpected bliss! O Pylades, Thou best of friends, thou kind protector, haste, Let us begone.

Pylades: [To his attendants.] Take off those shameful bonds; [They take off her chains.] Fall from her hands, ye chains, for they were made To wield a sceptre.

SCENE VIII.

Electra, Iphisa, Pylades, Pammenes.

Electra: O Pammenes, where, Where is my Orestes, my deliverer? Why comes he not?

Pammenes: This is a dreadful moment, And full of terror, for his father's spirit Demands a sacrifice, and justice waits To pay it, so hath heaven decreed: this tomb Must be the altar where the victim's blood Shall soon be shed; that sacred duty done, He will attend thee; but thou must not see A sight so terrible: thou knowest the laws Of Argos suffer not thy spotless hands To join with her ere the appointed time.

Iphisa: But say, Pammenes, what of Clytemnæstra, How acts she in this dreadful crisis?

Pammenes: Vainly She deprecates the wrath of fierce Orestes, And strives to save Ægisthus; kneels for pardon, And craves that boon she never will obtain: Meantime the furies, deaf to her entreaties, And thirsting for the cruel murderer's blood, Throng round Orestes, and demand his life.

Iphisa: O may this day of terror be a day Of pardon and forgiveness; may it finish The cruel woes of our unhappy race! Hark, Pylades, Electra, heard ye not A dreadful groan?

Electra: My mother's sure.

Pammenes: 'Tis she.

Clytemnæstra: [Behind the scenes.] O spare me!

Iphisa: Heaven!

Clytemnæstra: [Behind the scenes.] My son!

Electra: He kills Ægisthus. O hear her not, Orestes, but go on, Revenge, revenge, dissolve the horrid tie, And sacrifice the murderer in her arms: Strike deep.

Clytemnæstra: My son! O, thou hast slain thy mother.

Pylades: O cruel fate!

Iphisa: O guilt!

Electra: O wretched brother! Crimes punish crimes; forever be this day Lamented by us!

SCENE IX. Orestes: [Enters.] Open wide, thou earth, And swallow me: O Clytemnæstra, Atreus, And Tantalus, I come, I follow you To Erebus, a partner in your crimes, To share your tortures.

Electra: O what hast thou done?

Orestes: She strove to save him, and I smote them both— I can no more—

Electra: She fell then by thy hand! O dreadful stroke! and couldst thou—

Orestes: 'Twas not I; 'Twas not Orestes; some malignant power Guided my hand, the hateful instrument Of heaven's eternal wrath: Orestes lives But to be wretched; banished from my country, When my dear father fell, my mother slain, And by my hand; an exile from the world, Bereft of parents, country, fortune, friends, Now must I wander: all is lost to me: O thou bright orb, thou ever glorious sun, Shocked at our crimes, and Atreus's horried feast, Thou didst withdraw thy beams, and yet thou shinest On me! O wherefore in eternal night

Dost thou not bury all? O tyrant gods, Merciless powers, who punished me for guilt Yourselves commanded, O for what new crime Am I reserved? speak—ye pronounce the name Of Tauris, there I'll seek the murderous priestess, Who offers blood alone to the angry gods, To gods less cruel, less unjust than you.

Electra: Stay, and conjure their justice and their hate.

Pylades: Where'er the gods may lead, thy Pylades Shall follow still, and friendship triumph o'er The woes of mortals, and the wrath of heaven.

End

[1]Nothing could add more to the horror of the crime than such a circumstance. Clytemnæstra, not content with murdering her husband, instituted a solemn feast in commemoration of the happy event, and called it, with cruel raillery, "the supper of Agamemnon" Dinias, in his *History of Argos*, informs us, it was on the thirteenth of the month Gamelion, which answers to the beginning of our January.

www.ingramcontent.com/pod-product-compliance
Lightning Source LLC
Chambersburg PA
CBHW031434040426
42444CB00006B/807